HAPPY BIRTHDAY

Today is Scott's Birthday.
He is four years old
One-two-three-four.
Scott! Good for you.

Scott sees a lot of boxes on the chair. They are wrapped in fancy paper and tied with bright ribbons.

What can they be? "Open them, Scott," says Mother. "They are your presents from the family." Here is the birthday boy with all his presents on the floor around him.

Is there a train? Yes! It is from Daddy, and he wants to play with it, too.

Is there a whistle?
Yes! A blue one from Sister. She is putting it on a blue ribbon so that Scott can wear it.

Is there a sailboat? Oh, yes! The boat is from Mommie. "You may sail it in your bath now," She tells Scott.

Is there a ball and bat? Yes, a small one. Big Brother says, "That's from me, Scott. I'll teach you how to play.

Suddenly the doorbell rings. It rings again, and again and again.

Scott runs to the front door. "Happy Birthday!" shout all his friends. They have come to Scott's birthday party

Each one has a little present and they watch as Scott opens his packages.

They build a train with Scott's big blocks. Toot! Toot!

They play ring-around-the-rosy and they all fall down!
Ho! Ho!

They all go into the birthday party. Scott sits down at the head of the table.

Everyone has hats.
Everyone has snappers
Everyone has candy.

Everyone has fun.
Everyone sings
Happy Birthday:

Happy Birthday

Happy Birthday, Happy Birthday
 Happy Birthday to you.
Happy Birthday, Happy Birthday
 Happy Birthday to you.
And good wishes and blessings
 for your happiness, too.
Happy Birthday, Happy Birthday
 Happy Birthday to you.
Happy Birthday, Happy Birthday
 Happy Birthday to you.

Then out go the lights . . . In comes the cake! One-two-three-four bright candles, and one extra for good luck. And now Scott is really four years old!

Everyone sings!

Here's a birthday cake
Happy, happy birthday cake,
Mommie made it just for you
Happy, happy birthday cake,
Now you blow the candles out
Blowing, blow the candles out,
All your wishes will come true
When you blow the candles out.
Now it's time to cut that cake
Happy, happy birthday cake,
Give a piece to all your friends
Happy, happy birthday cake.
Now it's time to cut that cake
Golly gee, it tastes so good,
Golly gee, it tastes so good
Happy, happy birthday cake.

Happy Birthday to you, Happy Birthday to you.
Happy Birthday, Happy Birthday, Happy Birthday to you.

And now Scott takes a deep breath and blows with all his might. Poof! Out go ALL the candles.

www.ingramcontent.com/pod-product-compliance
Lightning Source LLC
Chambersburg PA
CBHW051216290426
44109CB00021B/2478